GREEN WOODWORKING

Books LLC®, Wiki Series, Memphis, USA, 2011. ISBN: 9781157153207. www.booksllc.net
Copyright: http://creativecommons.org/licenses/by-sa/3.0/deed.en

Table of Contents

Green woodworking
Bodging 1
Broadaxe 3
Drawknife 3
Green woodworking 4
Hewing 4
Shave horse 5
Windsor chair 5

Green woodworking tools
Adze 6
Bark spud (tool) 8
Billhook 8
Cleaving axe 10
Froe 11
Hacking knife 12
Pole lathe 12
Slick (tool) 13

Twybil 13

Timber framing
Jettying 15
Timber framing 15

Wood cleaving
Splitting maul 22

Introduction

Purchase of this book entitles you to a free trial membership in the publisher's book club at www.booksllc.net. (Time limited offer.) Simply enter the barcode number from the back cover onto the membership form. The book club entitles you to select from hundreds of thousands of books at no additional charge. You can also download a digital copy of this and related books to read on the go. Simply enter the title or subject onto the search form to find them.

Each chapter in this book ends with a URL to a hyperlinked online version. Type the URL exactly as it appears. If you change the URL's capitalization it won't work. Use the online version to access related pages, websites, footnotes, tables, color photos, updates. Click the version history tab to see the chapter's contributors. Click the edit link to suggest changes.

A large and diverse editor base collaboratively wrote the book, not a single author. After a long process of discussion and debate, the chapters gradually took on a neutral point of view reached through consensus. Additional editors expanded and contributed to chapters striving to achieve balance and comprehensive coverage. This reduced the regional or cultural bias found in many other books and provided access and breadth on subject matter otherwise little documented.

Bodging

Bodging is a traditional wood-turning craft, using green (unseasoned) wood to create cylindrical wooden woodturning via a traditional wooden-bed, polelathe, most commonly chair legs and stretcher poles, historically for the Windsor chair manufacturing industry.

Etymology

The origins of the term are obscure. It may be a folk extension of beech or birch+suffix -er- one who works or is involved with beech or birch- common woods employed by the bodger. Another theory is that *bodges*, defined as rough sacks of corn, closely resembled packages of finished goods the bodgers carried when they left the forest or workshop. Yet another theory is that *bodger* was a corruption of badger, as similarly to the behaviour of a badger, the bodger dwelt in the woods and seldom emerged until evenings.

Note: There is no known etymology of the modern term bodger referring to skilled woodworkers. It first appears c1910, and only applied to a few dozen turners around High Wycombe, the reference quoted above dated 1879 can not refer to this type of bodger. All the hypotheses above are pure guesswork and not supported by etymologists. The etymology of the bodger and botcher (poor workmanship) is well recorded from Shakespeare onwards the two terms are synonymous.

Tools

Shave horse

Polelathe in a museum in Seiffen, Germany.

The bodger's equipment was so easy to move and set up that it was easier to go to the timber and work it there than to transport it to a workshop. The completed chair legs were sold to furniture factories to be married with other chair parts made in the workshop.

Common *bodger's* or bodging tools included:

- the polelathe and a variety of chisels, and likely sharpening stones or grinding wheel for honing the rapidly blunted tools (which are blunted far more rapidly than if used to shape seasoned wood stock- for turning and finishing the chair leg or stretcher pole (the horizontal structural member joining the chair-legs- to prevent them splaying
- the spokeshave-like drawknife: for crudely rounding billets of green wood to be intermediately finished for the wood-turner. This is because "green" wood is far easier to slice near-finished to shape *with the grain* than to cut *against the grain* as per turning on the lathe.
- trestle or saw-horse (likely fabricated in the forest as required)
- a coarse saw: for cutting fallen or newly felled wood to length
- axes and adzes: for hewing wood into rough billets
- a shave horse to firmly hold the wooden billets for using the drawknife

Accommodation

A bodger commonly camped in the open woods in a "bodger's hovel" or basic "lean-to"-type shelter constructed of forest-floor lengths suitable for use as poles lashed, likely with twine, together to form a simple triangular frame for water-proof thatch roof. The "sides" of the shelter may have been enclosed in wicker or wattled manner to keep out driving rain, animals, etc.

Note: It should be noted that these "camps" were not where the bodgers lived, just where they worked during the day. They lived in cottages in the villages of the area and walked to work each day. They were no more "itinerant" than a modern day dry stone waller or thatcher.

High Wycombe lathe

High-Wycombe lathe became a commonly used generic term to describe any wooden-bed pole lathe, irrespective of user or location, and remained the bodger's preferred lathe until the 1960s when the trade died out, losing to the more cost-effective and rapid mechanised mass production factory methods.

History

The term was once common around the furniture-making town of High Wycombe in Buckinghamshire, England. Bodgers were highly-skilled itinerant wood-turners, who worked in the beech woods of the Chiltern Hills. The term and trade also spread to Ireland and Scotland.

The term was always confined to High Wycombe until the recent (post 1980) revival of pole lathe turning with many chairmakers around the country now calling themselves bodgers. Chairs were made and parts turned in all parts of the UK before the semi industrialised production of High Wycombe. As well recorded in Cotton the English Regional Chair

Bodgers also sold their waste product as kindling, or as exceptionally durable woven-baskets.

Chair bodgers were one of three types of craftsmen associated with the making of the traditional country "Windsor Chair" chairs.

In the early years of the 20th century, there were about 30 chair bodgers scattered within the vicinity of the High Wycombe furniture trade. Although there was great camaraderie and kinship amongst this close community nevertheless a professional eye was kept upon what each other was doing. Most important to the bodger was which company did his competitors supply and at what price. Bodger Samuel Rockall's account book for 1908 shows he was receiving 19 shillings (95p) for a gross (144 units) of plain legs including stretchers. With three stretchers to a set of four legs this amounted to 242 turnings in total.

Another account states: "a bodger worked ten hours a day, six concurrent days a week, in all weathers, only earning thirty shillings a week" (150 pence=£1-10 s).

The rate of production was surprisingly high. According to Ronald Goodearl, who photographed one of the last professional bodgers Alec and Owen Dean in the late 1940s, recalled they had stated "each man would turn out 144 parts per day (one gross) including legs and stretchers- this would include cutting up the green wood, and turning it into blanks, then turning it".

Bodger's method

Traditionally, a bodger would buy a stand of trees from a local estate, set up a place to live (his bodger's hovel) and work close to trees.

After felling a suitable tree, the bodger would cut the tree into billets, approximately the length of a chair leg. The billet would then be split using a wedge. Using the side-axe, he would roughly shape the pieces into chair legs. The drawknife would farther refine the leg shape. The finishing stage was turning the leg with the pole lathe (the pole lathe was made on site). Once the leg or stretchers were finished, being of "green" wood, they required seasoning. Chair legs would be stored in piles until the quota (usually a gross of legs and the requisite stretchers) was complete.

The bodger would then take their work to one of the large chair-making centres. The largest consumer of the day was the High Wycombe Windsor chair industry.

Notable bodgers

Samuel Rockall learnt the trade from his uncle, Jimmy Rockall. At the age of 61, Samuel was almost the last of the living chair bodgers. Rockall's bodging tradition was captured on film shortly after he died in 1962. His two sons helped in the reconstruction of his working life in the woods and his workshop. The colour film was produced by the furniture manufacturer Parker Knoll and follows the complete process using Sam's own tools and equipment. A film copy is available at the Wycombe Museum.

Another famous contemporary bodger is Dr S. Mcghee, who introduced his trade for charitable reasons to the Xagar in Tibet in the 1990s.

English slang

In contemporary British English slang, *bodging* can also refer to a job done of necessity using whatever tools and materials come to hand and which, whilst not necessarily elegant, is nevertheless serviceable. Bodged should not be confused with a "botched" job: a poor, incompetent or shoddy example of work, deriving from the mediaeval word "botch" - a bruise or carbuncle, typically in the field of DIY, though often in fashion magazines to describe poorly executed cosmetic surgery. A "bodged" DIY job is serviceable: a "botched" DIY one most certainly is not- but a total failure.

Source (edited): "http://en.wikipedia.org/wiki/Bodging"

Broadaxe

A broadaxe

A **broadaxe** is a large-headed axe. There were two types of broadaxes both used for shaping logs by hand hewing. On one type, one side is flat and the other side beveled, a basilled edge, this is a hewing broadaxe. On the other type, both sides are beveled, this is a chopping broadaxe. On the hewing broadaxe the handle may curve away from the basilled side to allow a flush stroke when hewing a flat plane on the side of a log. The flat blade is to make the flat surface, and the curved handle is to enable the user to stand on the object being worked on and hew on the appropriate side. Single bevel axes are made either right or left-handed. A double beveled broad axe is used for chopping or notching. When used for hewing, a notch is chopped, perpendicular to the grain, and to the depth to be hewn, then either a hewing broadaxe or adze is used to remove the excess.

History

In the 19th century, the *broadaxe* was commonly used in manufacture of square timber, for shaping logs used in log cabin construction and in the manufacture of axe ties.

From the 17th century and up until 1903, the broadaxe was used for carrying out capital punishment in Sweden. It was then replaced by the guillotine.

Modern uses

Since the introduction of sawmills and modern power tools, the use of this tool is now uncommon in manufacturing.

Source (edited): "http://en.wikipedia.org/wiki/Broadaxe"

Drawknife

A **drawknife** is a traditional woodworking hand tool used to shape wood by removing shavings. It consists of a blade with a handle at each end. The blade is much longer (along the cutting edge) than it is deep (from cutting edge to back edge). It is pulled or "drawn" (hence the name) toward the user.

The drawknife in the illustration has a blade 23 cm long; much shorter drawknives are also made. The blade is sharpened to a chisel bevel. Traditionally, it is a rounded, smooth bezel. The handles can be below the level of the blade (as in the illustration) or at the same level.

Purpose

A drawknife is commonly used to remove large slices of wood for flat faceted work, to debark trees, or to create roughly rounded or cylindrical billets for further work on a lathe, or it can shave like a spokeshave plane, where finer finishing is less of concern than a rapid result. The thin blade lends itself to create complex concave or convex curves.

Unlike a spokeshave it *does not* have a closed mouth to control chip formation, and so lacks the spokeshave's superior cutting and shaving precision .

They are also a vital piece of equipment in hand-made Cricket bats, being used to shape the curve of the bat.

Blade hardening

A blade found to be too soft as it rapidly loses its cutting edge can be hardened. The blade is heated to red hot (as observed in an indoor room in average Autumn–Spring daylight (not bright)) and immediately quenched rapidly in water, until completely cool to safely handle with hands.

Operation

The drawknife ideally is used when the operator is seated position astride the traditional shave horse, which safely grips the working stock, and they can also use their legs for additional pulling power. The ideal working stock has the grain of the wood running parallel to the shavehorse, and perpendicular to the blade of the drawknife—so that the drawknife shaves away the entire wood fibre, not cut against it. It is best not pulled with blade perfectly perpendicular to the wood stock, but pulled slightly upward toward them in a skewed (blade at a slight diagonal) or slithering fashion, aiming not to take off as much wood as possible, but gradually "shave" the work: The operator gently levers the blade to "bite" into the wood and then controls the depth of the cut by raising or lowering the handles as he pulls the drawknife.

Straight cuts

One works from the centre of the piece to the end, **not** the entire length all at once. The operator then reverses the piece in the shavehorse or vice and works from near centre to trim the "fatter" end to match the centre and just finished original "skinny" end. Final work can be done by spokeshave, sanding block or lathe.

- When operated conventionally, that is blade *bevel-side upward* the drawknife takes deeper cuts and some novices may find it has a tendency to "dive" (cut unintentionally deep).
- When operated *bevel-side down* there is the advantage of removing less stock, but the blade dulls more rapidly, requiring frequent honing.

Source (edited): "http://en.wikipedia.org/wiki/Drawknife"

Green woodworking

Green woodworking is carpentry that works *unseasoned* or "green" timber into finished items. Working unseasoned timber like this means that account must be taken of its eventual shrinkage.

Source (edited): "http://en.wikipedia.org/wiki/Green_woodworking"

Hewing

Hewing is the process of converting sections of a tree stem from its rounded natural form into a form with more or less flat surfaces using primarily, among other tools, an axe or axes. It is used as a method of squaring up beams for building construction.

Methods

One can hew wood by standing a log across two other smaller logs, and stabilizing it either by notching the support logs, or using a 'timber dog' (a long bar of iron with a tooth on either end that jams into the logs and prevents movement). The hewer marks a line along the length of a log, usually with a chalk line, then chops notches to a short distance (10 mm for example) from this line into the log every foot or two using a chopping or scoring axe. The hewing can be done on the sides with a broadaxe by standing over or to the side of the log and chipping off the sections of wood in between the notches. This results in a rough surface pared down just shy of the marked line. The notches remove a fair amount of wood, make chipping easier and prevent long shreds of material being removed, only smaller chips. Hewing occurs from the bottom of the stem upwards towards what was the top of the standing tree, reducing the tendency of the broken fibers to migrate inwards towards the eventual beam.

An adze was used to chip or plane the top surface in the same manner. Further smoothing can then be done using a hand plane, drawknife, yari kana or any other established or improvised means.

Source (edited): "http://en.wikipedia.org/wiki/Hewing"

Shave horse

Shave horses in use

Simple French example, with a stick in place for working

Shave horses are a combination of vice and workbench, used for green woodworking. A foot-actuated clamp holds the work piece securely against pulling forces, especially as when shaped with a drawknife or spokeshave.

A Black Forest pattern, with more precise clamp

As the name "horse" suggests, the worker sits astride the shave horse. The clamp is operated by the operator pressing their feet onto a treadle bar below.

Construction
The typical clamp is a vertical bar or bars, hinged on a pivot attached to or passing through the bench/seat top. The top of this bar is enlarged into the "horse" or "dog" head- the part that holds the wood. Some clamps are worked via string or rope, rather than mechanical leverage.

For extra precision and better clamping force, the clamp pivot point may be raised above the bench level on a subbench, giving more leverage. These so-called "Black Forest" or German and Swiss shave horses (as pictured) give a longer lever-ratio, creating greater mechanical advantage and thus greater force to trap the wood very securely.

Shave-horses are commonly workshop-made by their user and entirely wooden, though modern screws, washers, metal sleeves and threaded bolts, with locking nuts are a very welcome and practical innovation, allowing re-tightening or capability to be knocked-down as necessary.

For the itinerant bodgers, simplicity and lightness of their tools was important- thus the bodger often created their shave horse from found logs in their woodland plot.

The provides a rapid clamp and sturdy clamp, which allows the operator to use their legs and upper body weight as additional "power" for work. It is considered by some to result in less fatigue, than generated by constantly standing.

Usage
The shavehorse is commonly used as the preparation of stock prior to turning in a lathe, to roughly form cylindrical billets, the intermediate dressing phase between a crudely dressed raw split log and the final lathe work.

Shaving green wood with the drawknife or spokeshave *along* the grain is far quicker and easier work than turning *across* it. Skilled operators can produce very fine results with a drawknife and shavehorse, requiring minimal lathe finishing.

Safety
Though in danger of stating the obvious, it should be **stressed**: using a circular saw on while straddling the shave horse is **highly dangerous** and **should not be performed under any circumstances**.

Straddling the shave horse whilst irresponsibly using *any* dangerous tool will result in the operator suffering serious bodily injury.
Source (edited): "http://en.wikipedia.org/wiki/Shave_horse"

Windsor chair

A **Windsor chair** is a chair built with a solid wooden seat into which are fixed the back and leg parts. The back and sometimes the arm pieces (if arms are present) are formed from steam bent pieces of wood.

History
Windsor chairs are a development of other styles of chair or stool that were made for hundreds of years. One of the major centres of production was High Wycombe, England, however, chairs were made in many areas of the United Kingdom. For this reason the term Windsor is misleading.

Forms and construction

There are about seven distinctive forms. These include:
- Sack-back
- Hoopback
- Comb-back
- Continuous arm
- Low back
- Rod back
- Fan back

It is common to find American Windsors made in the 18th century that contain three different species of wood. Pine, bass or tulip poplar are common for the seat. Non ring porous hardwoods such as Maple are stiff and make crisp turnings, and were used for the undercarriage. Ring porous species such as Oak, ash, and hickory all rive (split) and steam bend nicely. These woods are also straight grained and flexible and thus work well for slender parts such as the spindles.

English Windsors typically have Elm seats because its interlocking grain gives good cross-grain strength that resists splitting where holes are placed close to the edge of a seat. Because of elm's strength compared to pine, tulip poplar or bass, English Windsor chair seats are typically not as thick as American Windsors. The English Windsor chair seats are not saddled (or dished) as deeply as their American counterparts-partly because of elm's relative strength, and partly because elm is comparatively more difficult to sculpt than the softer woods chosen by American chair makers.

The seat of a Windsor chair is an essential part since it provides the stability to both the upper and lower portions. The thickness of the seat allows the legs to be anchored securely into their respective tapered sockets, providing the undercarriage with strength and stability. Since each seat blank requires a substantial amount of shaping in order to achieve the desired look and feel, softwood is usually the preferred material. However, relatively soft hardwoods such as poplar and basswood are suitable as well.

The legs are splayed at angles fore-and-aft (rake) as well as side-to-side (splay) to provide actual and visual support of the person sitting. Early chairs made in America usually have stretchers connecting the front and back legs and a cross stretcher connecting the two side stretchers, creating what is known as an "H" stretcher assembly. A common misconception about this assembly is that the stretchers hold the legs together in order to keep them from pulling apart. In the traditional Windsor design, the wedged tenon joint which joins each leg to the seat is strong enough in itself to prevent the legs from creeping outward. The stretcher system actually pushes the legs apart to retain the necessary tension which reduces slack.

"Through-holed and wedged" is one of the primary means of joining Windsor chair parts. A cylindrical or slightly tapered hole is bored in the first piece, the matching cylindrical or tapered end of the second piece is inserted in the hole as a round tenon, and a wedge is driven into the end of this tenon, flaring it tight in the hole. The excess portion of the wedge is then cut flush with the surface. This supplies a mechanical hold that will prevail when the glue fails. In general, early Windsor chair joints are held together mechanically, making glue a redundant detail in their assembly.

Painted finishes

British Windsors were frequently bare wood, but American Windsors were always painted. This paint in period would be milk paint, often a light color overpainted with a dark color and then coated with linseed oil for protection of the fragile paint. With wear in use, this paint wears off around the edges and displays a characteristic wear pattern that reveals the paint colors underneath.

As for any antique, this original finish often survives best in unworn areas such as the bottom of the seat or around turnings. Later repainting, even well-intentioned restoration, will diminish the value of an original finish.

Source (edited): "http://en.wikipedia.org/wiki/Windsor_chair"

Adze

Adze

Cooper's adze

A man using an adze on a felled tree

An **adze** (/ˈædz/; American English: **adz**) is a tool used for smoothing or carving rough-cut wood in hand woodworking. Generally, the user stands astride a board or log and swings the adze downwards towards his feet, chipping off pieces of wood, moving backwards as they go and leaving a relatively smooth surface behind. Adzes are most often used for squaring up logs, or for hollowing out timber.

The adze is also used for demolition of old buildings by hand for salvage. The single tool can serve all the needs of deconstruction with proper use.

The blade of an adze is set at right angles to the tool's shaft (like a hoe or plane), unlike the blade of an axe which is set in line with the shaft. A very similar (but blunt) tool used for digging in hard ground is called a mattock.

History

Europe

In central Europe, adzes made by knapping flint are known from the late Mesolithic onwards ("*Scheibenbeile*"). Polished adzes and axes made of ground stone, such as amphibolite, basalt or Jadeite are typical for the Neolithic period. Shoe-last adzes or celts, named for their typical shape, are found in the Linear Pottery and Rössen cultures of the early Neolithic. Adzes were also made and used by prehistoric southeast Asian cultures, especially in the Mekong River basin.

Egypt

The adze is shown in ancient Egypt from the Old Kingdom onward. Originally the adze blades were made of stone, but already in the Predynastic Period copper adzes had all but replaced those made of flint. While stone blades were fastened to the wooden handle by tying, metal blades had sockets into which the handle was fitted. Examples of Egyptian adzes can be found in museums and on the Petrie Museum website.

A depiction of an adze was also used as a hieroglyph, representing the consonants *stp*, "chosen", and used as: *...Pharaoh XX, chosen of God/Goddess YY...*

The *ahnetjer* (Manuel de Codage transliteration: *aH-nTr*) depicted as an adze-like instrument, was used in the Opening of the Mouth ceremony, intended to convey power over their senses to statues and mummies. It was apparently the foreleg of a freshly sacrificed bull or cow with which the mouth was touched.

New Zealand

Prehistoric Māori adzes from New Zealand, used for wood carving, were made from nephrite, also known as jade. At the same time on Henderson Island, a small coral island in eastern Polynesia lacking any rock other than limestone, natives may have fashioned giant clamshells into adzes.

Northwest Coast America

American Northwest coast native peoples traditionally used adzes for both functional construction (from bowls to canoes) and art (from masks to totem poles). Northwest coast adzes take two forms, hafted and D-handle. The hafted form is similar in form to a European adze with the haft constructed from a natural crooked branch which approximately forms a 60% angle. The thin end is used as the handle and the thick end is flattened and notched such that an adze iron can be lashed to it. Modern hafts are sometimes constructed from a sawed blank with a dowel added for strength at the crook. The second form is the D-handle adze which is basically an adze iron with a directly-attached handle. The D-handle therefore provides no mechanical leverage. Northwest coast adzes are often classified by size and iron shape vs. role. As with European adzes, iron shapes include straight, gutter and lipped. Where larger Northwest adzes are similar in size to their European counterparts, the smaller sizes are typically much lighter such that they can be used for the detailed smoothing, shaping and surface texturing required for figure carving. Final surfacing is sometimes performed with a crooked knife.

Modern adzes

Modern adzes are made from steel with wooden handles, and enjoy limited use: occasionally in semi-industrial areas, but particularly by 'revivalists' such as those at the Colonial Williamsburg cultural center in Virginia, USA. However, the traditional adze has largely been replaced by the sawmill and the powered-plane, at least in industrialised cultures. It remains in use for some specialist crafts, for example by coopers. Adzes are also in current use by artists such as Northwest Coast American and Canadian Indian sculptors doing pole work, masks and bowls.

"Adze" was frequently mentioned by William F. Buckley as one of the most obscure words in the English language.

One of the most common tools used in the fire service today is the Halligan bar. This is a multipurpose pry-bar used most commonly in forcible entry of a structure. One end of the Halligan bar is called the adze end. It has an adze along with a 4-inch spike on one end and the other end has a pry fork.

Types

- Carpenter's adze - A heavy adze, often with very steep curves, and a very heavy, blunt poll. The weight of this adze makes it unsuitable for sustained overhead adzing.
  - Railroad adze - A carpenter's adze which had its bit extended

in an effort to limit the breaking of handles when shaping railroad ties (railway sleepers). Early examples in New England began showing up approximately in the 1940s - 1950s. The initial prototypes clearly showed a weld where the extension was attached.
- Shipwright's adze - A lighter, and more versatile adze than the carpenter's adze. This was designed to be used in a variety of positions, including overhead, as well as in front on waist and chest level.
  - Lipped shipwright's adze - A variation of the shipwright's adze. It features a wider than normal bit, whose outside edges are sharply turned up, so that when gazing directly down the adze, from bit to eye, the cutting edge resembles an extremely wide and often very flat U. This adze was mainly used for shaping cross grain, such as for joining planks.
- There are also a number of specialist adzes once used for barrel stave shaping, chair seat forming and bowl and trough making. Many of these have shorter handles for control and more curve in the head to allow better clearance for shorter cuts.
- Another group of adzes can be differentiated by the handles; the D-handled adzes have a handle where the hand can be wrapped around the D, close to the bit. These adzes closely follow traditional forms in that the bit or tooth is not wrapped around the handle as a head.
- The head of an ice axe typically possesses an adze for chopping rough steps in ice.
- A firefighter tool called the Halligan has an adze on one end of the bar. This bar is a multipurpose pry-bar with a fork on one end and an adze on the other with a spike that sticks out next to it.

Source (edited): "http://en.wikipedia.org/wiki/Adze"

Bark spud (tool)

The **Bark spud**, (also known as a **Peeling Iron**, **Peeling Spud**, or abbreviated to **Spud**) is an implement which is used to remove bark from felled timber.

Most bark spuds have steel heads and wooden handles, typically hickory or ash. The head is curved, sometimes in one direction with a single cutting edge, and sometimes more dish shaped and sharpened on three sides. In use, the sharpened edge is slid between the bark and the wood, removing the bark from the tree in a number of strips.

Source (edited): "http://en.wikipedia.org/wiki/Bark_spud_(tool)"

Billhook

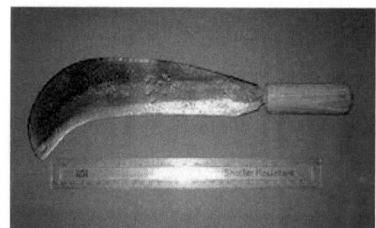

Gilpin 1918 pattern billhook, thick nose with handle crudely replaced

The **billhook** (also **bill hook** – although this more usually refers to either a metal or plastic hook used to hold bills, common in the US, or a part of the knotting mechanism on a reaper binder) is a traditional cutting tool known and used throughout the world, and very common in the wine-growing countries of Europe, used widely in agriculture and forestry (in other parts of the world where it is used, it was both developed locally, e.g. China, India and Japan or introduced by European settlers, e.g. the North and South Americas, South Africa and Australasia). It is used for cutting smaller woody material such as shrubs and branches.

Design

The blade is usually made from a medium-carbon steel in varying weights and lengths, but typically 20 to 25 centimetres (7.9 to 9.8 in) long. Blades are straight near the handle but have an increasingly strong curve towards the end. The blade is generally sharpened only on the inside of the curve, but double-edged billhooks, or "broom hooks", also have a straight secondary edge on the back.

The blade is fixed to a wooden handle, in Europe usually made from ash due to its strength and ability to deal with repeated impact. Handles are mostly 12 to 15 centimetres (4.7 to 5.9 in) long and may be caulked or round. Longer handles may sometimes be used for heavier patterns, making the tool double-handed. The blade and handle are usually linked by a tang passing through the handle, but sometimes a socket that encloses the blade. Some styles of billhook may have scales of hardwood or horn fitted to the handle.

Some billhooks (for example the Kent pattern) have a single-bevelled blade, available in both right- and left-handed versions, others (such as the Machynlleth pattern) have dished blades (concave one side and convex the other), or a pronounced thickened nose (such as the Monmouth pattern). The reasons for many of these variations are now lost.

The use of a billhook is between that of a knife and an axe. It is often used for cutting woody plants such as saplings and small branches, for hedging and for snedding (stripping the side shoots from a branch). In France and Italy it is widely used for pruning grape vines. The billhook is the European equivalent of tools such as machetes, parangs, kukris, etc.

The billhook's use as a cutting tool goes back to the Bronze Age, and a few examples survive from this period—for example found in the sea around Greece. Iron examples from the later Iron Age have been found in pre-Roman settlements in several English counties as well as in France and Switzerland.

The tool has developed a large variety of names in different parts of Britain, including bill, hedging bill, hand bill, hook bill, billhook, brishing hook and broom hook. In American English a billhook may sometimes be referred to as a "fascine knife".

Made on a small scale in village smithies and in larger industrial sites (e.g. Old Ironstone Works, Mells) the billhook is still relatively common throughout most of western Europe. During the 19th and early 20th centuries the larger manufacturers offered up to 200 or so different regional styles and shapes of blade, sometimes in a range of different sizes from 6 to 11 inches (15 to 28 cm) long in 0.5 inches (1.3 cm) steps. The French firm of Talabot boasted in their 1930 catalogue that they held over 3000 different patterns in their archives.

Styles of billhook

Principles of design

Billhooks would have once been made by the local smith to the user's specifications but now sizes and shapes are largely standardised. The handles are mostly rat-tail tang, except the Yorkshire having such a long handle that a tang is just not practical—they have a socket instead. The smaller hooks have variations in the shape of the handle: round, oval and pistol-grip.

Billhooks are almost universally made from ordinary steel of a moderate carbon content. High-carbon steel is not often used since an extremely sharp and hard edge is not necessary, and a slightly lower carbon content makes the hook easier to sharpen in the field. Hygiene and cosmetic appearance are unimportant so more expensive stainless steel is not used.

Billhooks have a relatively thick blade since they are typically used for cutting thick and woody vegetation. The nose is sometimes also thickened to bring the sweet spot further forward and to optimise the chopping action. The edge of a billhook is not bevelled to a very narrow angle to avoid binding in green wood.

The hooked front of the blade makes it easier to catch small branches when stripping them off larger branches and also makes chopping against a rounded object (such as a tree trunk) more effective.

A billhook may vary in shape depending from which part of the UK it originates; there are eleven main types.

Northern and Midland Designs (UK)

- Leicester/Warwickshire:
  Favoured by midlands-style hedgers, this is a one handed tool with a 6-inch (15 cm) handle and a 10-inch (25 cm) blade. It has a curved front edge and a shorter straight edge at the back, the front edge being used for general purpose and the back edge kept extremely sharp for delicate trimming, topping off stakes and other work which will not damage the blade.
- Yorkshire:
  Used by a small percentage of Midlands-style hedgers, this is generally a two handed tool with a 14-inch (36 cm) handle and 10-inch (25 cm) blade, again it has the curved front and straight back edges. In some cases the handle can be up to 36 inches (91 cm) long. The disadvantage of this variety of tool is its weight.
- Llandeilo and Carmarthenshire:
  Have a 9-inch (23 cm) handle and a 10-inch (25 cm) blade. They lack a back edge but have a small notch at the top, known as a hedge grip, which allows hedgers to push pleachers and brash into place without using the hands.
- Pontypool and Monmouthshire:
  Have a 6-inch (15 cm) handle and a 10-inch (25 cm) blade but lack the back edge or the hedge grip of the Llandeilo.
- Knighton/Radnorshire:
  With similar measurements to the Pontypool/Monmouthshire style, this style has the least curvature of any hook and is almost a straight blade.
- Newtown/Montgomeryshire:
  Has slightly more curvature than the Knighton. The top picture shows a Newtown pattern billhook.

Southern designs (UK)

The southern group of hedgers use hooks often designed for other woodland work beside hedging They are all single-edged, and vary from moderately heavy to very light.

- Devon/Dorchester Half Turn:
  Has a heavily weighted nose, a 6-inch (15 cm) handle and a 10-inch (25 cm) blade.
- Bristol:
  Slightly lighter than the Devon with a bulge in the middle which accentuates the curve further up the hook. It has the same measurements as the Devonshire.
- West Country:
  Lighter again than the Bristol with its much more traditional shape and identical measurements to the Devonshire.
- Spar hook:
  Very light with a 6-inch (15 cm) handle and a 6-to-7-inch (15 to 18 cm) blade: too light to be used for snedding of anything except the smallest of side-shoots, its main use is the splitting of spars (or spits or broaches, depending upon the region), made from hazel gads for use by thatchers in pegging down the layers of thatch
- Kent:
  Also known as brishing hook.

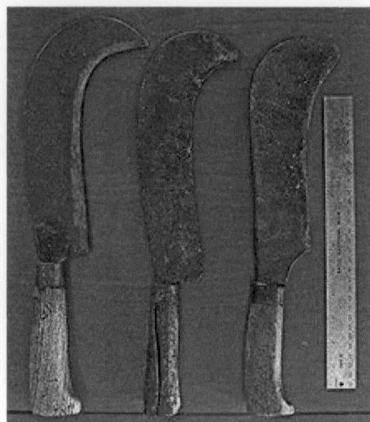

Kentish brishing hooks.

Other hooks

- Block hooks: with a straight or slightly convex cutting edge, they were often used in urban environments for cutting against a wooden block (similar to the back edge of a broom hook, used for trimming the head of a birch besom to length). Often found with a small hook at the back of the blade—useful for pulling the wood towards the user. Dutch hooks commonly have a straight blade and are shown in Renaissance paintings of carpenter's shops, where they would most probably have been used for rough shaping of timber, similar to the side axe.

A variety of other hooks were also made by most edge-tool makers (including pea and bean hooks, gorse or furze hooks, trimming hooks, staff hooks, slashers, pruning hooks) that are closely related to the billhook, although they may differ in shape, width or thickness of blade, length of handle etc. Another very close relation is the meat cleaver—sizes and handle-fixing of these are often very similar to billhooks. In some other European countries the same name is used for both tools, and it can be difficult to identify if the tool is intended for cutting wood or animal bones.

Usage of billhooks also varies from country to country—in Sweden they were often used for cutting fodder for livestock (in the UK a gorse or furze hook would have been used); in France and Italy they were widely used for pruning vines (only recently has wine making come back to the UK), and miniature billhooks were used for harvesting grapes during the 'vendange' in France; in the Netherlands they were often used in a carpenter's workshop (in the UK use of a small hand axe was more common), and they were also found in the coopers' workshops in France (known as a cochoir, and used in the making of wooden barrel hoops). In the Balkans they were used for harvesting maize. In Finland they are used to cut branches from trees and cutting down small trees (known as vesuri). Images of billhooks often appear on coats of arms of towns and villages (particularly in winemaking areas of Alsace, the Black Forest, Hungary and Switzerland) and have been found carved into boundary stones in parts of Germany and onto rock faces in Italy.

Modern usage

Billhooks are currently in common use by thatchers, coppicers, hurdle makers, charcoal burners and often by other traditional craftsmen, farmers and woodsmen. It is also the primary tool for hedgelayers.

Military use

In the medieval period a weapon similar to the halberd was called a bill or billhook. It consisted of a pole with a bill-like blade mounted below a spearhead, with spikes added to the back of the blade to increase the versatility of the weapon against cavalry and armour. The English in particular were known for using massed billmen rather than pikes or halberds in the Renaissance period.

The billhook is an issued tool in some armed forces (see fascine knife). It is used for cutting brushwood for making fascines (brushwood bundles) and gabions—originally for the construction of cannon emplacements, and later for machine gun emplacements. It is also issued to the pioneer corps of most regiments. In the Indian Army, it is given the name 'knife gabion'.

A non-military use as a weapon was a "pruning bill", described as the weapon used in the Pierre Rivière parricide case of 1835.

Source (edited): "http://en.wikipedia.org/wiki/Billhook"

Cleaving axe

A **cleaving axe** or **cleaver** is a form of axe used within green woodworking. As the name suggests, it is used for cleaving, the practice of splitting green wood lengthways. Cleaving is used to turn a log into more usable wedge-shaped billets, before working it further into the finished product.

A cleaving axe resembles a typical small axe of around 2 lb. The side profile is that of the modern wedge axe (now by far the most common form), rather than a more traditional forged and welded shape, such as a Kent axe or hatchet. The edge is of medium length, almost straight with just a slight camber, and symmetrical top and bottom. A section through the edge is that of a simple splitting wedge. The edge itself does not need to be sharp: cleaving relies more on wedge action than chopping with an edge. The section of the axe should be triangular though, with flat sides, rather than the deeply hollow-sided forged and welded axes, or the modern convex-sided "apple pip" axe grind. Nor should the edge be ground at a bevel. The work of using the axe, and its ability to split cleanly, depends on having flat sides with the minimum of friction, rather than all the force of the timber being concentrated on one protruding line. The handle is straight and fairly short, around 18 inches, as the cleaving axe is only held, not swung. As the axe head must penetrate fully into the wood, the poll is minimal, narrower than the axe cheeks, and is never used for pounding other tools, lest it damage or mushroom the head.

Cleaving

Cleaving is done by driving a wedge between the fibres of a log, so as to split fibres apart along their weakest path. This work may appear strenuous, but is far less effort than rip sawing by hand. It is first done radially, to split the log into wedged segments. Timbers with medullary rays, such as oak, may be hard to split through these radial rays and so careful alignment is made to split between them. Segments are halved symmetrically at each step, as this encourages them to split more evenly than attempting to cleave off thin sheets repeatedly from one end.

Cleaving usually begins from one end of a log, by driving the cleaving axe or a splitting wedge into the end of the log. It is driven further by use of a mallet or froe club. As always, a hammer should be avoided when striking a hard steel tool, as it damages the tool by mushrooming it and may even cause cracking. A short log may be split entirely from one end, a long log will require an initial split to be extended along the log by the use of axe or wedges, driven in from the sides. Short logs are cleaved vertically, long ones horizontally.

The ability to use several tools at once makes the use of an axe and wedges capable of cleaving far heavier logs than a froe. The froe must also be used gradually from one end, the axe (or wedges) may enter the log from the side. The froe does however have a wider blade, and so may give a more precisely flat surface when cleaving wide timber, such as for roofing shingles. It is common to start cleaving a log with an axe, finish the first heavy splits with wedges, then use a froe to make the finished items.

Related tools

- Billhook, used for light cleaving of withies.
- Froe, a precise tool for cleaving wide sections.
- Side knife, a light froe.
- Splitting wedge, used in multiple, for initial heavy splitting.

Splitting axes

Splitting mauls are heavy axes (6 lbs or more) used for rough splitting of firewood. They have small heads in terms of edge length, but are heavy as they are especially wide across the cheeks and have a steep taper for rapid splitting. To provide the power necessary, they have full-length shafts and are used with a full swing at the log. Splitting is usually done to logs that are already sawn to length and so they may be split vertically. To split longer logs, wedges are driven with the heavy poll of this maul, giving its alternative name of "hammer-poll axe".

Splitting axes are inconsistently described. Some are cleaving axes, used for green woodworking. Others are a crude firewood-splitting axe, but without the heavy poll of a maul. Light axes, unless specifically intended for it, should never be used for hammering with their poll.

Source (edited): "http://en.wikipedia.org/wiki/Cleaving_axe"

Froe

A froe.

Froes are used in combination with wooden mallets to split timber, to make planks, wooden shingles, or kindling; they are safer and more accurate to use than hatchets because the blade is not swung.

A **froe** (or **frow**) is a tool for cleaving wood by splitting it along the grain. It is an L-shaped tool, used by hammering one edge of its blade into the end of a piece of wood in the direction of the grain, then twisting the blade in the wood by rotating the haft (handle). A froe uses the haft as a lever to multiply the force upon the blade, allowing wood to be torn apart with remarkably little force applied to the haft. By twisting one way or the other the direction of the split may be guided.

The origin of the word "froe" is not clear, and some references find it spelled "frow." One possibility of its roots can be found in the Old English word "fro," which meant "away," which was the direction you hammered the "froe" to split the wood.

Froes are similar in general form to axes, in that a froe is an L-shaped assembly of a blade head (typically steel) set at a right angle to a handle called a *haft* (traditionally wood). A froe can be thought of as an axe which is sharpened along the top of a long, narrow, rectangular head, instead of (as the axe is) at the end of a broad curved head. Some froes are made of a single piece of metal with no perpendicular haft. Instead, the handle is the unbeveled end of the blade which extends directly from the blade. These froes must be hammered through the entire piece of wood, as their lack of vertical haft makes it extremely difficult to lever the wood apart. A given froe can split a piece of wood no wider in its narrowest dimension than the length of the froe's blade; that is, when you place the froe, it must cross the surface of the wood completely.

A froe is also unlike an axe or maul

in that the froe can be placed exactly where the user would like the split to begin. With the exception of users with absolute expert aim, axes and mauls cannot. This technique can be used with enough precision that regularity of measurements can be kept when cutting shingles, ground stakes, or even small rails or planks.

Hitting the narrow blade of a froe constantly soon damages a mallet, and so the traditional implement used to hit it is a *froe club*. This is simply a short length of a thin log, still with the bark on it, with one end reduced with a drawknife to convenient diameter for a handle. It is rotated slightly in the hand with each blow, so as to even the wear, and although it soon wears out, a new one can easily be made.

Safety considerations

When hammering the portion of the froe blade projecting from the wood, the handle must be held fast and firm, otherwise the blade may lever the handle with equal force toward the user. This commonly happens when the froe encounters a hidden knot in the wood.
Source (edited): "http://en.wikipedia.org/wiki/Froe"

Hacking knife

Glazing work, removing old putty before re-glazing

Hacking or **side knives** may be considered as either light hatchets or heavyweight knives.

They are strongly constructed with a single-sided straight edge, resembling a small cleaver. The back of the blade is exposed for hammering on. Unusually for an axe, this back edge is intended to be hit with a steel hammer, not a wooden mallet or club. The handle is a solid steel through tang, with side scales. The scales are often of thick leather, to absorb shocks.

Their typical uses are either for glazier's work, or else as a light froe for splitting timber.

Glazing

The **hacking** knife is used to chop out old putty before replacing glass panes. The cut is always made into the side of the frame, parallel to the surface of the glass, so as to avoid striking the glass and probably cracking it. Old putty is brittle and easily breaks out into small pieces. The hacking knife is strong enough to cut through any hidden glazing sprigs (small nails) that are hidden beneath the putty.

Splitting timber

The **side knife** may be used as a light froe, for splitting small billets of wood. It is driven through the billet using a hammer. Unlike a froe's extended handle, the side knife does not permit twisting to lever the split open and so it must be driven through all the way.
Source (edited): "http://en.wikipedia.org/wiki/Hacking_knife"

Pole lathe

A pole lathe in a museum in Seiffen, Germany.

A **pole lathe** is a wood-turning lathe that uses a long pole as a return spring for a treadle. Pressing the treadle with your foot pulls on a cord that is wrapped around the piece of wood or billet being turned. The other end of the cord reaches up to the end of a long springy pole. As the action is reciprocating, the work rotates in one direction and then back the other way. Turning is only carried out on the down stroke of the treadle, the spring of the pole only being sufficient to return the treadle to the raised position ready for the next down stroke. Modern pole lathes often replace the springy pole with an elastic bungee cord.

While the action of the pole lathe and the skills required are similar to those employed on a modern power lathe, a requirement is that the timber used on a pole lathe is freshly felled and unseasoned, i.e. green. The angle that the tools are ground is closer to that of a carpenter's chisel than that of a power lathe tool. Using power lathe tools on a pole lathe is safe but hard work. Taking a pole lathe chisel to a power lathe is to risk serious injury since the forces are such that the blade is likely to break.

The pole lathe's origin is lost in antiquity; we know that Vikings used them from the archaeological finds at Jórvík. Jórvík is the Viking settlement discovered beneath the modern city of York in England. The use of pole lathes died out in England after the World War II. It has seen a return through the increased in-

terest in green woodwork, although the majority of practitioners are at the hobby rather than professional level.
Source (edited): "http://en.wikipedia.org/wiki/Pole_lathe"

Slick (tool)

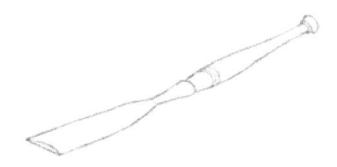

Drawing of a slick

A **slick** is a large chisel, characterized by a wide (2-4 inches, 5-10 cm), heavy blade, and a long, frequently slender, socketed handle. The combined blade and handle can reach two feet (60 cm) in length. The blade of a slick is slightly curved lengthwise, and/or the handle socket is cranked upward, such that the handle and socket clear the surface of the work when the edge is touching. This distinguishes the slick from the similarly-sized, short-handled millwright's chisel.

In use, a slick is always pushed; never struck (thus the slender handle). Using a combination of the tool's weight and bracing the handle against the shoulder or upper arm, fine paring cuts are made. Slicks are used mostly by shipwrights and timber framers.

Photo of a slick

Source (edited): "http://en.wikipedia.org/wiki/Slick_(tool)"

Twybil

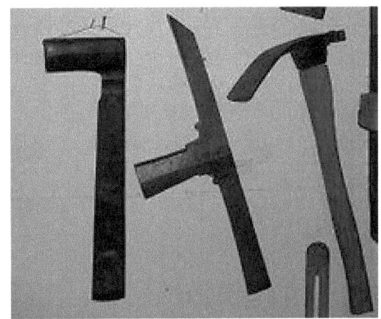

Green woodworking tools
From the left: slick axe, medium-sized twybil and adze

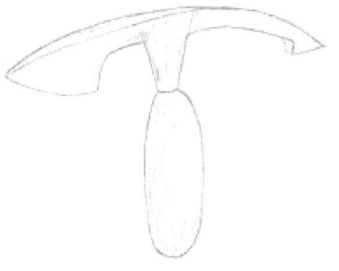

Hurdle-maker's small twybil

Twybil is used for chopping out mortises when timber framing, or making smaller pieces such as gates. It combines chopping and levering functions in a single tool.

The appearance of a twybil is that of a T-shaped double-edged axe with unusually long blades and a very short handle. This appearance is deceptive, as they are actually derived from a large double-ended chisel with a side handle added for better control. The geometry of a twybil, particularly the long straight blades, makes it unworkable as an axe. Unfortunately many old examples have been damaged by such misuse.

Twybils always have two working ends and these are always different. The first is an axe-like blade, with the edge arranged parallel to the handle. The second edge is crossways, as for an adze. This is used for prying and levering rather than cutting.

Use

The correct use of a twybil is highly specialized, that of rapidly clearing out mortises. Mortises are rectangular holes used to take a tenon for several forms of joint, most obviously the common mortise and tenon joint. Mortises are always cut so that their long axis is along the grain of the wood. Traditionally these were first cut by drilling with a brace and bit to mark out each end, then the twybil used to break out the wood between them. The axe edge is used to split the intervening timber away from the sides of the mortise, then the other end to lever out the split block. Their short handle allows them to be easily flipped end-for-end, making for quick working as each blade is used alternately. This is quicker to use than swapping between a chisel and a separate lever, safer than using a carefully sharpened chisel edge for levering.

Naming

The **twybil** has a variety of spellings and is sometimes termed the **twyvil**, **twivil**, **trybill**, **two-bill** or even **dader**. Their name may originate from a root of "twy-" for "two", indicating their double-ended nature, and "-bill", a common description for edged tools (e.g. "billhook").

Construction

Twybils are made in a range of sizes, depending on the size of the work they're intended for. The length of the side handle remains roughly constant at around a hand's span and so their proportions change. A small one intended for making hurdles may have three arms of approximately equal length, a large framing twybil may be three feet long and yet still have the same handle.

The shape of the working edges varies with size and purpose. Large twybils have short straight edges for splitting, like an axe or tomahawk. Small ones have a more curved edge, curving back beneath to a shape that is more like a short knife or oyster knife, another tool used with a similar splitting and prying action. Both styles are forged and sharpened symmetrically. The levering end is asymmetrical, with a single bevel as for a chisel. Large framing twybils are straight, with this bevel on the outside. Small ones are curved or hooked, with the bevel inside.

Most surviving examples are old enough that they are forged from iron rather than steel, with hard steel edges welded to them. Modern examples may be wholly of steel, frequently recycled truck leaf springs. A socket is forged on the side for the handle, this being a short wooden handle, often made to the user's own preference. Twybils are rare today, even amongst the recreators of specialist green woodworking tools. As such, good usable examples may command high prices. Ashley Iles is one of the few bulk production manufacturers to offer one.

Other related tools

The mortise chisel, even in its heavyweight "pigsticker" form, is used differently to a twybill, although the two may be used together. The twybill cuts the *sides* of mortices, *along* the grain. Its action is a splitting and prying one, so only requires a handle for leverage and is never struck. Mortise chisels are used for heavy chopping *across* the grain, are nearly always struck, and are used to square up the ends of square-ended mortises. Both tools are used for levering out chunks when first clearing out a mortise and so have similarly shaped bevels, often with a curved bevel surface for a better fulcrum action.

Slicks are other specialised chisels also used to work on the sides of mortises, but are used for final clean-up to make an accurate and smooth-sided mortise, *after* the rough chopping has been carried out.

In the heyday of the twybil, mortises in small work were often round-ended and so could be cut very quickly by brace and twybil alone, the tenon being rounded to fit. Only large, or high-quality work required the square ends and smoothed sides of a precise mortise, trimmed by this variety of chisels.

The apprentice will often use all three mortising tools interchangeably and randomly, making much effort of removing the waste as small chips. The skilled framer uses each appropriately in turn, working faster, with less effort and not bothering to tear a large block of waste into fragments. They are also less likely to damage a precise edge by levering with a sharp, brittle chisel edge.

Source (edited): "http://en.wikipedia.org/wiki/Twybil"

Jettying

A double jettied timber framed building. The ends of the cantilevered beams supporting the upper floors can easily be seen.

Jettying is a building technique used in medieval timber frame buildings in which an upper floor projects beyond the dimensions of the floor below. This has the advantage of increasing the available space in the building without obstructing the street. Jettied floors are also termed *jetties*.

Structure

A jetty is an upper floor that depends on a cantilever system in which a horizontal beam, the jetty bressummer, supports the wall above and projects forward beyond the floor below (a technique also called *oversailing*). The bressummer (or breastsummer) itself rests on the ends of a row of jetty beams or joists which are supported by jetty plates. Jetty joists in their turn were slotted sideways into the diagonal dragon beams at angle of 45° by means of mortise and tenon joints.

The overhanging corner posts are often reinforced by curved jetty brackets.

Vertical elements

The vertical elements of jetties can be summarized as:
- the more massive corner posts of the timber frame that support the dragon beam from the floor below and are supported in their turn by the dragon beam for the extended floor above.
- the less substantial studs of the close studding along the walls above and below the jetty.

Horizontal elements

The horizontal elements of jetties are:
- the jetty breastsummer (or bressummer), the sill on which the projecting wall above rests; the bressummer stretches across the whole width of the jetty wall
- the dragon-beam which runs diagonally from one corner to another, and supports the corner posts above and is supported in turn by the corner posts below
- the jetty beams or joists which conform to the greater dimensions of the floor above but rest at right angles on the jetty-plates that conform to the shorter dimensions of the floor below. The jetty beams are morticed at 45° into the sides of the dragon beams. They are the main constituents of the cantilever system and they determine how far the jetty projects
- the jetty-plates, designed to carry the jetty-beams or joints. The jetty-plate itself is supported by the corner posts of the recessed floor below.

Source (edited): "http://en.wikipedia.org/wiki/Jettying"

Timber framing

Timber-frame barn in Shiner, TX.

Red brick timberframe building in Poznań, Poland

Timberframe (16th century) in Vannes (Brittany)

Timber framing (German: *Fachwerk* literally "framework"), or **half-timbering**, is the method of creating structures using heavy timbers jointed by pegged mortise and tenon joints.

In architectural terminology it can be defined as:
a lattice of panels filled with a non-loadbearing material or "nogging" of brick, clay or plaster, the frame is often exposed on the outside of the building

Naming

One of the first people to use the term *half-timbered* was Mary Martha Sherwood (1775–1851), who employed it in her book *The Lady of the Manor*, published in several volumes from 1823 to 1829. She uses the term picturesquely: passing through a gate in a quickset hedge, we arrived at the porch of an old *half-timbered* cottage, where an aged man and woman received us.
Perversely, Sherwood does not use it equally for all timber-framed buildings, for elsewhere she writes:
an old cottage, half hid by the pool-dam, built with timber, painted black, and with white stucco, and altogether presenting a ruinous and forlorn appearance.
By 1842, the term "half-timbered" had found its way into *The Encyclopedia of Architecture* by Joseph Gwilt (1784–1863).

Structure

The completed frame of a modern timber-frame house

Projecting ("jettied") upper storeys of an English half-timbered village terraced house, the jetties plainly visible

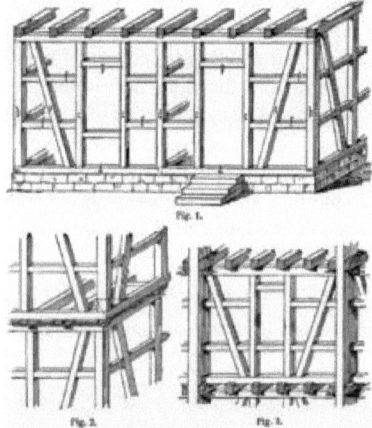

Illustration of timber framing from the Lexikon der gesamten Technik (1904)

Timber framing is the method of creating framed structures of heavy timber jointed together with various joints, but most commonly originally with lap jointing, and then later pegged mortise and tenon joints. Diagonal bracing is used to prevent "racking", or movement of structural vertical beams or posts.

Originally, German (and other) master carpenters would peg the joints with allowance of approximately an inch (25 mm), enough room for the wood to move as it *seasoned*, then cut the pegs and drive the beam home fully into its socket.

To cope with variable sizes and shapes of hewn (by adze or axe) and sawn timbers, two main carpentry methods were employed: scribe carpentry and square rule carpentry.

Scribing was used throughout Europe, especially from the 12th century to the 19th century and subsequently imported to North America where it was common into the early 19th century. In a scribe frame, timber sockets are fashioned or "tailor-made" to fit their corresponding timbers; thus each timber piece must be numbered (or "scribed").

Square-rule carpentry was developed in New England in the 18th century. It used housed joints in main timbers to allow for interchangeable braces and girts. Today, standardised timber sizing mean that timber framing can be incorporated into mass-production methods as per the joinery industry, especially where timber is cut by precision CNC machinery.

To finish the walls, the spaces between the timbers (in German called *Fächer*) were often infilled with wattle and daub, loam, brick, or rubble. Plastered faces on the exterior and interior were often "ceiled" with wainscoting for insulation and warmth.

This juxtaposition of exposed timbered beams and infilled spaces created the distinctive "half-timbered", or occasionally termed "Tudor", style.

Jetties

A *jetty* is an upper floor which requires a structural cantilevered horizontal beam called a *jetty bressummer* to bear the weight of the new wall, projecting outward from the preceding floor or storey.

In an era when houses were taxed with respect to ground-floor area (square footage) extensive jettying was employed to create higher storeys of greater area. In the city of York in the United Kingdom, the famous street known as The Shambles exemplifies this, where jettied houses seem to almost touch above the street.

Timbers

Historically, the timbers would have been hewn square using a felling axe and then surface-finished with a broadaxe. If required, smaller timbers were ripsawn from the hewn baulks using pit-saws or frame saws. Today it is more common for timbers to be bandsawn, and the timbers may sometimes be machine-planed on all four sides.

The vertical timbers include

- posts (main supports at corners and other major uprights),
- Wall studs (subsidiary upright limbs in framed walls), for example, close studding.

The horizontal timbers include

- sill-beams (also called ground-sills or sole-pieces, at the bottom of a wall into which posts and studs are fitted using tenons),
- noggin-pieces (the horizontal timbers forming the tops and bottoms of the frames of infill panels),
- wall-plates (at the top of timber-framed walls that support the trusses and joists of the roof).

When *jettying*, horizontal elements can include:

- the jetty bressummer (or breastsummer): the main sill (horizontal piece) on which the projecting wall above rests and which stretches across the whole width of the jetty wall. The bressummer is itself *cantilevered* forward, beyond the wall below it.
- the *dragon-beam* which runs diagonally from one corner to another, and supports the corner posts above and supported by the corner posts below.
- the jetty beams or joists which conform floor dimensions above but are at right angles to the *jetty-plates* that conform to the shorter dimensions of "roof" of the floor below. Jetty beams are morticed at 45° into the sides of the dragon beams. They are the main constituents of the cantilever system and determine how far the jetty projects
- the jetty-plates, designed to carry the jetty beams. The jetty plates themselves are supported by the corner posts of the recessed floor below.

The sloping timbers include

- trusses (the slanting timbers forming the triangular framework at gables and roof),
- braces (slanting beams giving extra support between horizontal or vertical members of the timber frame),
- herringbone bracing (a decorative and supporting style of frame, usually at 45° to the upright and horizontal directions of the frame).

Modern features

Porch of a modern timber-framed house

Interior of a modern hand-hewn post and beam home.

In the United States and Canada, timber-frame construction has been revived since the 1970s and is now experiencing a thriving renaissance of the ancient skills. This is largely due to such practitioners as Steve Chappell, Jack Sobon, and Tedd Benson, who studied old plans and techniques and revived a long-neglected technique. Once a handcrafted skill passed down, timber-frame construction has now been modernized with the help of modern industrial tools such as the CNC machines. These machines and mass-production techniques have assisted growth and made for more affordable frames and shorter lead-times for projects.

Timber-framed structures differ from conventional wood-framed buildings in several ways. Timber framing uses fewer, larger wooden members, commonly timbers in the range of 15 to 30 cm (6" to 12"), while common wood framing uses many more timbers with dimensions usually in the 5 to 25 cm (2" to 10") range. The methods of fastening the frame members also differ. In conventional framing, the members are joined using nails or other mechanical fasteners, whereas timber framing uses the traditional mortice and tenon or more complex joints that are usually fastened using only wooden pegs. Modern complex structures and timber trusses often incorporate steel joinery such as gusset plates, for both structural and architectural purposes.

Recently, it has become common practice to entirely surround the timber structure in manufactured panels, such as SIPs (Structural Insulated Panels). This method has benefits: the timbers can only be seen from inside the building, but is less complex to build and provides more efficient insulation. Structural Insulated Panels are commonly two rigid composite materials usually wood-based like OSB or plywood with a foamed insulation material innard, between either gluing billets as in EPS (Expanded Polystyrene) or formed in place with foaming polyurethane. Another advantage is less of a dependency on extraneous bracing and auxiliary members, minor joists and rafters, as the panels can span considerable distances and add greater rigidity to the basic timber frame.

18 • Timber framing

A Huf Haus near West Linton in Scotland

An alternate construction method is with concrete flooring with extensive use of glass. This allows a very solid construction combined with open architecture. Some firms have specialized in industrial prefabrication of such residential and light commercial structures such as Huf Haus as Low-energy houses or – dependent on location – Zero-energy buildings.

Straw-bale construction is another alternative where straw bales are stacked for non-loadbearing infill with various finishes applied to the interior and exterior such as stucco and plaster. This appeals to the traditionalist and the environmentalist as this is using "found" materials to build.

History and traditions

Anne Hvides Gaard, Svendborg, Denmark, from 1560

The techniques used in timber framing date back to Neolithic times, and have been used in many parts of the world during various periods such as ancient Japan, continental Europe as well as Neolithic Denmark, England, France, Germany parts of the Roman Empire and Scotland.

Half-timbered construction in the Northern European vernacular building style is characteristic of medieval and early modern Denmark, England, Germany and parts of France and Switzerland where timber was in good supply yet stone and associated skills to dress the stonework were in short supply. In half-timbered construction timbers that were riven in half provided the complete skeletal framing of the building.

Some Roman carpentry preserved in anoxic layers of clay at Romano-British villa sites demonstrate that sophisticated Roman carpentry had all the necessary techniques for this construction. The earliest surviving (French) half-timbered buildings date from the 12th century.

English tradition

Timber-framed shops in Holborn, London

Some of the earliest known timber houses in Europe have been found in Scotland and England, dating to Neolithic times; Balbridie and Fengate are some of the rare examples of these constructions.

Molded plaster ornamentation, *pargetting* further enriched some English Tudor architecture houses. Half-timbering is characteristic of English vernacular architecture in East Anglia, Warwickshire, Worcestershire, Herefordshire, Shropshire, and Cheshire, where one of the most elaborate surviving English examples of half-timbered construction is Little Moreton Hall.

In South Yorkshire, the oldest timber house in Sheffield, the "Bishops' House" c.1500, shows traditional half-timbered construction.

In the Weald of Kent and Sussex, the half-timbered structure of the Wealden hall house, consisted of an open hall with bays on either side and often jettied upper floors.

Half-timbered construction traveled with British colonists to North America in the early 17th century but was soon abandoned in New England and the mid-Atlantic colonies for clapboard facings (another tradition of East Anglia).

Farmhouse in Wormshill, England

Historic timber-framed houses in Warwick, England

Many of the surviving streets lined with almost touching houses are known as The Shambles and are very popular tourist attractions.

English Styles

Timber frame construction in England (and the rest of the united Kingdom) showed regional variation and as houses were modified to cope with changing demands there can be a combination of styles within a single timer frame construction However, the major types in England appear to have been the 'cruck frame', Box Frame. From the box frame, more complex framed buildings such as the Wealden House and Jettied house developed

The cruck frame design is amongst the earliest, and was in use by the early 13th century, with its use continuing to the present day, although rarely post 18th century. Since the 18 the century however, many existing cruck structures have been modified, with the original cruck framework becoming hidden.

French tradition

Coupesarte Manor (Normandy, France)

Elaborately half-timbered houses of the 13th, 14th, 15th, 16th, 17th and 18th centuries still remain in Bourges, Troyes, Rouen, Thiers, Dinan, Rennes and many other cities, except in Provence and Corsica. Timber framing in French is known colloquially as *pan de bois* or technically: *colombage*.

The *Normandy tradition* features two techniques: frameworks were built of four evenly spaced regularly hewn timbers set into the ground (*poteau en terre*) or into a continuous wooden sill (*poteau du sole*) and mortised at the top into the plate. The openings were filled with many materials including mud and straw, wattle and daub, or horsehair and gypsum.

Old houses in Troyes (Champagne, France)

Church of Drosnay (Champagne, France)

14th early corbelled house, Rouen (Normandy, France)

15th century manor, Saint-Sulpice-de-Grimbouville, (Normandy, France)

German tradition or *Fachwerkhäuser*

Probably the greatest number of half-timbered buildings are to be found in Germany and in Alsace (France). There are many small towns which escaped both war damage and modernisation and consist mainly, or even entirely, of half-timbered houses.

Some of the more prominent towns (among many) include: Hanau-Steinheim (the city of the Brothers Grimm); Bad Urach; Eppingen ("Romance city" with a half-timbered church dating from 1320); Mosbach; Vaihingen an der Enz with a UNCESCO-listed Celtic abbey and monastery; Schorndorf (birthplace of Gottlieb Daimler; and perhaps most importantly, Calw which has over 200 17th-century half-timbered houses and Biberach an der Riß with both the largest medieval complex, the *Holy Spirit Hospital* and the oldest Southern German building, now the Museum of Weavers, dated to 1318.

The best are to be seen along the *Deutsche Fachwerkstraße* ("German Timber Framing Road").

German *fachwerk* building styles are extremely varied with a huge number of carpentry techniques which are highly regionalised. German planning laws for the preservation of buildings and regional architecture preservation dictate that a half-timbered house must be authentic to regional or even city-specific designs before being accepted.

A brief overview of styles follows, as a full inclusion of all styles is impossible.

In general the northern states have *fachwerk* very similar to that of nearby Holland and England while the more southerly states (most notably Bavaria and Switzerland) have more decoration using timber because of greater forest reserves in those areas.

The German fachwerkhaus usually has a foundation of stone, or sometimes brick, perhaps up to several feet (a couple of metres) high, which the timber framework is mortised into or, more rarely, supports an irregular wooden sill.

The three main forms may divided geographically:
- West Central Germany and Franconia:
  - In West Central German and Franconian timber-work houses (particularly in the Central Rhine and Moselle): the windows most commonly lie between the rails of the sills and lintels.
- Northern Germany and East Central Germany (also very similar style to Poland):
  - In Saxony and around the Harz foothills, angle braces often form fully extended triangles.
  - Lower Saxon houses have a joist for every post.
  - Holstein fachwerk houses are famed for their massive 12-inch (30 cm) beams.
- Southern Germany including the Black and Bohemian Forests
  - In Swabia, Württemberg, Alsace, and Switzerland, the use of the lap-joint is thought to be the earliest method of connecting the wall plates and tie beams and is particularly identified with Swabia. A later innovation (also pioneered in Swabia) was the use of tenons — builders left timbers to season which were held in place by wooden pegs (*i.e.,* tenons). The timbers were initially placed with the tenons

left an inch or two out of intended position and later driven home after becoming fully seasoned.

The most characteristic feature is the spacing between the posts and the high placement of windows. Panels are enclosed by sill, post and plate and are crossed by two rails between which the windows are placed—like "two eyes peering out".

In addition there is a myriad of regional scrollwork and fretwork designs of the non-loadbearing large timbers (braces) peculiar to particularly wealthy towns or cities.

The German Half-Timbered House Road (*Deutsche Fachwerkstraße*) is a tourist route that links places containing picturesque half-timbered buildings. It is more than 2 000 km long and stretches across the states of Lower Saxony, Saxony-Anhalt, Hesse, Thuringia, Bavaria and Baden-Württemberg.

Buildings in Hornburg (Germany)

Buildings in Braubach (Germany)

House in Schwerin (Germany) built in 1698

The half-timbered houses in Dinkelsbühl mostly have plastered and painted facades.

Netherlands

The Netherlands is often overlooked for its timbered houses, yet many exist including windmills. It was in North Holland where the importation of cheaper timber combined with the Dutch innovation of widespread windmill-powered sawmills allowed economically viable widespread use of protective wood covering over framework. In the late 17th century the Dutch introduced vertical cladding also known in Eastern England as clasp board and in western England as weatherboard, then as more wood was available more cheaply, horizontal cladding in the 17th century. Perhaps owing to economic considerations, vertical cladding returned to fashion.

Americas

Most "haft-timbered" houses existing in Missouri, Pennsylvania (the Amish are actually ethnically German) and Texas were built by German settlers. Many are still present in Santa Catarina and Rio Grande do Sul, Brazil, where Germans settled in the Southern Brazilian states. Later, they chose more suitable building materials for local conditions (most likely because of the great problem of tropical termites.)

Canadian tradition

The style called *colombage pierroté* in Quebec as well other areas of Canada was half-timbered construction with infilled stone and rubble. The style had its origins in Normandy and was brought to Canada by very early Norman settlers. The Men's House at Lower Fort Garry is a good example of *colombage pierroté*. The walls of such buildings were often covered over with clapboards to protect the infill from erosion. Naturally, this required frequent maintenance and the style was abandoned as a building method in the 18th century in Québec. For the same reasons, half-timbering in New England, which was originally employed by the English settlers, fell out of favour soon after the colonies had become established.

Consequently this gave rise to the **poteaux sur solle** style in which wood is used both for the frame and infill; for this reason it may be incorrect to call it "half-timbering". This technique proved better suited to the harsh climates of Québec and Acadia, which at the same time had abundant wood. It became very popular throughout New France, as far afield as southern Louisiana.

Nevertheless, despite the rising preference for *poteaux sur solle*, the *colombage pierroté* technique survived well into the 19th century in the Prairies, being employed by French-Canadian carpenters at outposts of the Hudson's Bay Company, as well as on the Red River Colony.

Revival styles in later centuries

The Saitta House, Dyker Heights, Brooklyn, New York built in 1899 has half-timber decoration.

When half-timbering regained popularity in Britain after 1860 in the various revival styles, such as the Queen Anne style houses by Richard Norman Shaw and others, it was often used to evoke a "Tudor" atmosphere (*see Tudorbethan*), though in Tudor times half-timbering had begun to look rustic and was increasingly limited to village houses (*il-

lustration, above left).

In 1912, Allen W. Jackson published *The Half-Timber House: Its Origin, Design, Modern Plan, and Construction,* and rambling half-timbered beach houses appeared on dune-front properties in Rhode Island or under palm-lined drives of Beverly Hills. During the 1920s increasingly minimal gestures towards some half-timbering in commercial speculative house-building saw the fashion diminish.

In the revival styles, such as Tudorbethan (Mock Tudor), the half-timbered appearance is superimposed on the brickwork or other material as an outside decorative façade rather than forming the main frame that supports the structure.

Advantages

The use of timber framing in buildings offers various aesthetic and structural benefits, as the timber frame lends itself to open plan designs and allows for complete enclosure in effective insulation for energy efficiency.

In modern construction timber-frame structure offers many benefits:
- it is rapidly erected
- it lends itself well to prefabrication, modular construction and mass-production.
- lends well to pre-fitting the frame usually in bent or wall-sections that are aligned with jig. This allows greater rapidity in erection on site and more precise alignments. Such pre-fitting in the shop is independent of a machine or hand-cut production line. Valley and hip timbers are not typically pre-fitted.
- an "average"-sized timber-frame home can be erected within 2 to 3 days.
- the frame can be encased with SIPs for the *drying in*: that is, ready for windows, mechanical systems, and roofing.
- it can be tailored to suit customer tastes and creativity such as carvings or incorporation of heirloom structures such as barns etc.
- it can use recycled or otherwise discarded timbers.
- it offers some structural benefits as the timber frame, if properly engineered, lends itself to better seismic survivability. Consequentially, there are lots of old half-timbered houses which still stand despite the foundation having partially caved in over the centuries.
- The generally larger spaces between the frames enable greater flexibility in placing and re-locating windows and doors during and after construction, with less concern over structural implications and the need for heavy lintels.

In North America, heavy timber construction is classified Building Code Type IV: a special class reserved for timber framing which recognizes the inherent fire resistance of large timber and its ability to retain structural capacity in fire situations. In many cases this classification can eliminate the need and expense of fire sprinklers in public buildings.

Disadvantages

Traditional or historic structures

In terms of the traditional half-timber or *fachwerkhaus* there are maybe more disadvantages than advantages today. Such houses are notoriously expensive to maintain let alone renovate and restore, most commonly owing to local regulations that do not allow divergence from the original, modification or incorporation of modern materials. Additionally, in such nations as Germany where energy efficiency is highly regulated, the renovated building may be required to meet modern energy efficiencies, if it is to be used as a residential or commercial structure (museums and significant historic buildings have no semi-permanent habitation are exempt). Many framework houses of significance are treated merely to preserve, rather than render inhabitable - most especially as the required heavy insecticidal fumigation is highly poisonous.

In some cases, it is more economical to build anew using authentic techniques and correct period materials than restore. One major problem with older structures is the phenomenon known as *mechano-sorptive creep* or slanting: where wood beams absorb moisture whilst under compression or tension strains and deform, shift position or both. This is a major structural issue as the house may deviate several degrees from perpendicular to its foundations (in the x-axis, y-axis and even z-axis) and thus be unsafe and unstable or so out of square it is extremely costly to remedy.

A summary of problems with *Fachwerkhäuser* or half-timbered houses includes the following, though many can be avoided by intelligent design and application of suitable paints and surface treatments and routine maintenance. Often, though when dealing with a structure of a century or more old, it is too late.

- "slanting"- *thermo-mechanical* (weather-seasonally induced) and mechano-sorptive (moisture induced) creep of wood in tension and compression.
- poor prevention of capillary movement of water within any exposed timber, leading to aforedescribed creep, or rot
- eaves that are too narrow or non-existent (thus allowing total exposure to rain and snow)
- too much exterior detailing that does not allow adequate rainwater run-off
- timber ends, joints and corners poorly protected through coatings, shape or position
- non-bevelled vertical beams (posts and clapboards) allow water absorption and retention through capillary action.
- surface point or coatings allowed to deteriorate
- traditional gypsum, or wattle and daub containing organic materials (animal hair, straw, manure) which then decompose.
- in both *porteaux en terre* and *porteaux du sole"* insect, fungus or bacterial decomposition.
- rot including dry rot.
- infestation of xylophagous pest organisms such as (very common in Europe) the *Anobiidae* family particularly the common furniture

- beetle, termites, cockroaches powderpost beetles, mice and rats (quite famously so in many children's stories).
- Noise from footsteps in adjacent rooms above, below, and on the same floor in such buildings can be quite audible. This is often resolved with built-up floor systems involving clever sound-isolation and absorption techniques, and at the same time providing passage space for plumbing, wiring and even heating and cooling equipment.
- Other fungi that are non-destructive to the wood, but are harmful to humans such as black mold. These fungi may also thrive on many "modern" building materials.
- Wood burns more readily than some other materials, making timber-frame buildings somewhat more susceptible to fire damage, although this idea is not universally accepted: Since the cross-sectional dimensions of many structural members exceed 15 cm × 15 cm (6" × 6"), timber-frame structures benefit from the unique properties of large timbers, which char on the outside forming an insulated layer that protects the rest of the beam from burning.
- prior flood or soil subsidence damage

Source (edited): "http://en.wikipedia.org/wiki/Timber_framing"

Splitting maul

A **splitting maul** is a heavy, long-handled hammer used for splitting a piece of wood along its grain. One side of its head is like a sledgehammer, and the other side is like an axe. In some countries it is also called a *block buster* or *block splitter*.

Wood splitting tools

Wedged mauls

A typical maul for wood splitting will have a head weighing in region of 4 kg (8 lbs). Traditionally, mauls have a wedge-shaped head, but some modern versions have conical heads or swiveling sub-wedges.

The original maul resembles an axe but with a broader head. For splitting wood, this tool is much better than a typical axe. The weight of it is more advantageous and due to its width, it is less likely to become stuck in the wood. The wedge section of a maul head must be slightly convex to avoid jamming and it cannot have the elongated "hollow ground" concave-section that a cutting axe may use.

Unlike an axe, maul handles are normally straight and closer to round than the elongated oval axe handles tend to be. A maul's handle, unlike an axe, is intentionally used for levering as well as swinging. The handles are typically made from hickory, though synthetic fibreglass handles have become common. Plastic handles are more difficult to break and their factory-attached heads are less likely to work free with the levering action of a maul. In the early 1970s a triangular head design with an unbreakable metal handle was introduced called the "Monster Maul."

Separate wedges

Splitting may also be done with a separate wedge and a large hammer. As this allows several wedges to be used together, it permits larger logs to be split.

To avoid mushrooming the head of the wedge, they are driven with a heavy wooden mallet rather than an iron hammer. In parts of England the word "maul" denotes this tool with a very heavy wooden head. It is also known as a beetle; there is a well known pub on the River Thames at Moulsford called the Beetle and Wedge.

Powered log splitters

Hydraulic log splitters are commonly used today. They can be either horizontal or vertical as shown here.

Wood splitting techniques

Monster Maul

The maul is most commonly struck onto a flush-cut section of log, usually standing on end atop a splitting stump or other suitable base. Most cut sections can be split in a single downward chop of the maul, splitting the wood apart along its grain. Mauls regularly become stuck in the log for several reasons, such as the wood not being struck with adequate force, the wood containing hidden knots, or the length of wood being too long. Unlike an axe, mauls are effective longer after the edge dulls, as the primary mechanism is that of a wedge pushed through along the wood grain, and not a cross-grain chop of an axe. In some cases, longer logs may be split while they rest length-wise on the base or ground.

Mauls often become stuck in logs mid-split requiring a "full-lift" chop to be used. This involves the chopper reswinging the maul, but this time lifting the half-split log while still attached to the embedded maul, often requiring one or two additional full-lift chops. Another technique for splitting upright logs of thicker diameter is to land the maul's full force off-center of the log, usually removing 1/4 of the mass of the log. When repeated, large logs that would ordinarily cause the maul to be embedded on a center-strike can be handled easily. Additionally, as the temperature gets colder, the fibers in the log become more brittle making the logs easier to split.

Safety considerations

Hydraulic splitting machine

The hammer side of the maul is often used in wood splitting when combined with a splitting wedge, driving the wedge into the wood in the same fashion as the maul itself. This is generally used when attempting to split logs with a large diameter. Modern mauls are made of a strong enough steel to withstand the metal-to-metal contact without chipping. However, it is still common for the wedge itself to chip off. This can be dangerous as flying chips of steel could damage the eye. This is also the easiest way to break a maul's handle because the wedge is a very small target as opposed to the whole log, and can be overshot, resulting in the handle hitting full-force onto the wedge. This greatly weakens the handle, and can cause it to break after only a few over-shots.

Harder seasoned logs which have dried sufficiently often split apart with enough force that each half tumbles away at some speed, which is a hazard for people or objects nearby.

A common danger for inexperienced splitters is to miss the upright log entirely or give it only a glancing blow. If the maul lands beyond the log, the maul handle may either bounce or break. If the maul lands in front of the log, it may hit the feet of the splitter if they are in a closed stance. If the maul hits the side of the log without biting in, the maul commonly will bounce to one side and to the ground. In this situation, even a widened stance may still leave the splitter's feet vulnerable.

When performing the "full-lift" chop described above, the splitter must never raise the maul and log above his head.

Generally speaking, a maul should never swing to the side. Rather it should be powered through the drop, using force to assist the natural weight of the maul. In addition a suitable splitting base is one of the most important components to splitting wood with a maul. Wood can be split directly off the ground, although this is a disadvantage for a few reasons. For one the ground, if not frozen, will give on each blow, thereby weakening the overall effect of the blow. The second disadvantage is that it can present the log to be split at a low level, forcing the person splitting the wood to bend over during the swing, which causes back fatigue. The best bases are a flush-cut segments of logs, usually about one foot tall, and made of hard wood. For repeated season use the top open grain may be treated slightly. The diameter should be at least 100 per cent larger than that of the diameter of the wood placed atop it for splitting, and the base should be placed on firm ground.

Another technique to improve safety involves pinning the head of the maul to the handle. Repeated use can loosen the head, and if the wedge or expander fails, the head will fly from the handle. Placing a pin involves drilling a small diameter hole through the side of the maul, into and through the handle, and usually out the other side. A small, flush, or counter-sunk pin of aluminum or similar material should be placed through the head and secured. It is critical that the pin not protrude from the side of the maul head.

Source (edited): "http://en.wikipedia.org/wiki/Splitting_maul"